The Unexpected Journey

The Unexpected Journey

AN INSPIRING TRUE STORY

Peggy Watrous Walters

PALMETTO
PUBLISHING
Charleston, SC
www.PalmettoPublishing.com

© 2024 Peggy Watrous Walters
All rights reserved.
No portion of this book may be reproduced,
stored in a retrieval system, or transmitted in
any form by any means–electronic, mechanical,
photocopy, recording, or other–except for
brief quotations in printed reviews,
without prior permission of the author.

Hardcover ISBN: 979-8-8229-5716-9
Paperback ISBN: 979-8-8229-5717-6
eBook ISBN: 979-8-8229-5718-3

CHAPTER 1

I am four and a half years old and I have just been told that I will have to spend a week or more away from my mother. Yikes! I can feel the fear creeping into my body. I have never spent a night away from my mother. Grandpa has to go into the hospital for a procedure, and Grandma wants me to stay with her.

ॐ

My mother's parents, Carmine and Angelina, are Italian immigrants from a small town south of Naples, Italy called Acerra. They were promised to one another by their parents when they were children.

For my grandmother, Angelina, life in Italy was easy. Her parents owned a plantation. They had several servants helping with the grounds, cooking, and housekeeping. She had a personal maid who looked after her wardrobe, kept her clothes clean and pressed, her hair styled, and assisted in all her bathing. Not many families in her town could afford such a lavish lifestyle. So, it was not surprising that she would be desirable as a future wife to any of the families with young boys at that time.

Carmine, on the other hand, came from a working family of entrepreneurs in the coffee business. There were times in his father's business that required him to work in Brazil on a coffee plantation, where Carmine would live as a young boy.

Carmine came to America in his late teens when his older half-brother, Francesco, sent for him. Francesco was in America working in Chicago on the railroad and was able to get Carmine a job. Both brothers worked hard to save money to send for their intended brides. Two brothers to marry two sisters.

Carmine adapted to America easily. Living in Brazil with his father as a boy made adjusting to different cultures easier. The time he had spent in the Calvary during World War I helped him learn the English language and speak it fluently. Grandma, however, resisted the American culture. She did not speak English very well, which limited her communication skills. I was to be her companion and interpreter. "Why me?" I had asked. I was the youngest of the girls. Surely, it would make more sense for one of my older sisters to go. But, no, Grandma wanted me.

I loved my grandmother. She was the typical grandmother figure back in the 1950s era. Medium height, plump, silver, short curly hair that was permed, silver-rimmed glasses, and black shoes laced high just below the ankle with seamed nylon stockings rolled down. She wore a loose-fitting dress with an apron. She had a quiet spirit about her brought on, I am sure, by my dominating grandfather. She was kind and loving with a forgiving nature. I saw no problem staying with Grandma. My fear was being away from my mother.

The day finally came that I would go. A small bag was packed with clothing, and another with some coloring books and a few small toys. Not many. Uncle John, my mother's brother, would be picking me up and taking me to Grandma's. My parents did not own a car. Living in the city near all the public transportation systems did not require an automobile. Mother did not ride with us. She stayed home with the other children.

We arrived at Grandma's house early in the day. She was happy to see us. She had been cooking, and the aromas from the kitchen could be smelled as you walked into the house. It was a small one-bedroom home with a large living and dining room. It had a nice eat-in kitchen with stairs leading to the basement. There was an enclosed staircase to the attic in the hall close to the dining room, which could be made into another bedroom. The attic was cool during the winter months. My grandfather loved to keep his wine on the steps to chill. As children, we were always allowed a small glass of wine for our Sunday dinners at their house. They would put a phone book on my chair for me to sit on so I could reach the table.

My uncle stayed for a short visit, enjoying the minestrone soup Grandma had prepared for our lunch, and then he left. He wanted to stop by the hospital to check on my grandfather.

My first day with Grandma went well, considering I did not speak or understand the Italian language very well. One minor detail everyone had overlooked in choosing me as a companion for Grandma. Mother did not speak Italian to us growing up. She would only use some Italian phrases. She wanted us to speak English in preparation for school. Poor Grandma. She had to repeat what she wanted me to do over and over, with pantomime. I had to make a dozen trips down to the basement trying to find just the right pot she needed to make our dinner. "No, no," she would say, signaling me to return to the basement. "La pen tola."

When nighttime fell, it was time for me to go to bed. Grandma had a big double bed compared to the twin bed I was used to sleeping in at home. The bedroom was modestly furnished and decorated.

The vintage of the furniture, I would guess, was from the 1920–30s. There was a highboy dresser for Grandpa and a nice low dresser for Grandma with a round frameless mirror attached. Tucked in between the mirror glass and the backing of the mirror were some family photos, a plastic rose flower on a stem, and a plastic embossed 8" x 10" picture of the bust of Jesus. A rosary hung on one of the mirror fasteners. There was a ceiling light fixture that hugged the ceiling, giving off a soft dim light. One of Grandpa's shirts hung from the back of an armchair. Next to the bed was a nightstand with a small lamp and a box of tissues. To anyone else, this would be considered a nice, cozy, comfortable room. To me, it was scary and lonely. I was used to sharing a bedroom with my two older sisters, each of us having our own twin bed and a dresser to share. I had never slept in a room all by myself. I knew that Grandma would eventually join me when it was time for her to retire, but for now, I would be alone.

I tried to be brave as she tucked me in and said good night in Italian. Then the light went out, and the door closed. My heart was pounding fast. I started to imagine the furniture turning into all kinds of creatures and that they were coming at me. The longer I lay there, the creatures became more real. I closed my eyes, but that only made it worse. Finally, I could not hold back my tears any longer, and my sobs turned into screams of panic.

Soon, Grandma came rushing into the bedroom with a concerned, puzzled look. What was wrong? Was I suddenly sick and in pain? No, I was scared and frightened of the dark and being alone, and I did not know how to communicate that to her. I continued to cry softly as she felt my forehead and placed her hand on my stomach. I shook my head from side to side to indicate I was not in pain or sick. She reached up to the dresser mirror and pulled out the plastic picture of Jesus. She cuddled it, spoke something in Italian, and gave it to me to hold and snuggle with. I looked at the 8" x 10" face of Jesus. The soft, reassuring smile on His face and kind eyes made me feel safe, and I did not feel alone anymore. My fear left as I took the picture in my arms. From that moment on, I knew I had a friend. What I did not know was that the friendship would last for life.

℘

The rest of the week went well. I spent time helping Grandma with her routine chores of cooking, cleaning, and shopping. Eventually, I did learn some Italian and our communication improved. I still find myself using some Italian words and phrases to this day.

I enjoyed having Grandma's company all to myself. I felt special not having to share her with anyone, including my mother. There was no competition, and the fear of sleeping alone went away because I was not alone anymore. I had Jesus. When it was time to go home, she helped me pack. She made sure I had my Jesus picture, and with her gentle smile and a few Italian words, she reached up to the mirror on her dresser and gave me the plastic rose as a going-away present.

Once home, I was greeted by my mother and older sister, Sharon. It was late in the evening, and my other sister and brother were already in bed. While preparing for bed, I shared my days spent with Grandma…the grocery shopping and dragging a grocery bag almost as big as me along the sidewalk walking home; the toys she made for me out of household items like an empty spool of thread, clothes pin, and an empty box of napkins that became a house for toy people who were really clothes pins standing along the spool table. Grandma's imagination and creativity were something I never saw in her before. When she and Grandpa would come to visit, her time was spent in the kitchen cooking with Mother. How kind, I thought, that she would take the time to entertain me. I enjoyed her company. She kept me busy with light house chores, which made the time pass. Mother was interested in my stories and the picture of Jesus. She, like Grandma, tucked it in the mirror in my bedroom.

CHAPTER 2

My parents, Edward and Gloria, were a hardworking middle-class couple. Mother was the only surviving daughter born to my grandparents. She had a sister who died as an infant, an older brother, John, and a younger brother, Frank. She could do no wrong in the eyes of my grandfather, unlike his sons, who endured strict discipline. Grandpa was hard on the boys. Especially his youngest son, Frank, who was always getting into mischief. Frank loved to provoke Grandpa and get him fired up. Grandma always came to his rescue. John, on the other hand, had a serious nature. He was an obedient, responsible boy who was favored by Grandpa. He went to a trade school and became an aeronautical engineer. Frank had many careers, his last being an electrician working for the city.

My father is the eldest of three sons born to his parents, Paul and Marie. He had two brothers, Paul and Richard. They lived a hard life raised by his grandmother, often doing without the things most children have. His parents divorced when the boys were young. His father spent many hours working as a tool and die maker. He was very good at his craft and made a good living. However, he also was a big spender, leaving very little for his sons. All three boys served in the armed forces during World War II. Dad was in the Army. His unit was attached to General Patton's.

Both my parents were raised in Chicago on the southwest side, where ethnic neighborhoods were developed by immigrants like my grandparents. Most everyone lived in an apartment or two-flat. It was a luxury to own your own home at the time my parents were growing up. The Great Depression affected most middle-income families. Thousands of jobs were lost, making it difficult to live.

Grandpa was a tailor by trade, working in a haberdashery shop selling men's clothes and accessories. When sales began to fall because no one was buying new clothes, Grandpa had to find another way to make a living to provide for his family. During those depression years, my grandfather became a "jack of all trades." He did anything he could to provide for his family…shoe repair, door-to-door sales, real estate sales…anything to earn an income. He applied for HUD housing and moved his family into a new affordable luxury apartment called the Mary Jane Projects. This housing still exists today.

Apartment living was confining. Families often gathered at parks for picnics and outdoor entertainment. This is how my mother met my dad. After school they would go to Douglas Park's recreational building and play ping pong and other games. As Mother tells the story, Dad chased her until she finally gave up. World War II kept them apart for a while, but they eventually got together again and got married.

My parents struggled financially, raising five children. Finding a suitable, affordable apartment with five children was not an easy task. Rents were based on how many children you had. That made my parents' housing expense more than most families. But, like most middle-class families, home ownership was not an option, at that time.

My first apartment as a child was above a small grocery store that housed multiple apartments. Then, when I was four years old, we moved into a two-flat. It was much larger and more spacious, with a large living and dining room, eat-in kitchen, three bedrooms, and a bath. Our apartment was on the first floor, which gave us access to the basement. The renters above us had to use the outside entrance to the basement for the laundry facilities. While we had the convenience of an interior entrance to the basement, we also had the responsibility of keeping the building heated in the winter. That meant making sure the furnace had plenty of coal. When our dad was not around, my sisters and I took on that task.

The basement was a dark, creepy place used mostly for storage. In the winter, my mother would have us help her hang the clothes on clotheslines that hung from the rafters. There were two storage areas, one for each tenant, and a room where the coal was delivered across from the furnace. The laundry area was separate and close to the rear entrance, so the tenant on the second floor had easy access to the sinks and washers. My older sisters and I would often do the laundry to help Mother. It was an old washing machine on wheels with a laundry tub and rollers on top to remove the excess water. My grandfather stored his wine barrels there. He made excellent peach brandy. While a basement would be a perfect place to play, especially during the winter months, we never did. It was a scary place to be.

The neighborhood we lived in was once a wealthy neighborhood. The streets were lined with tall, white, stone two-story buildings. Garfield Park and the conservatory were within walking distance. Grandpa loved to take us there while my mother and grandma would be preparing meals. We would walk around the park, and Grandpa would push us on the swings. The elementary school we attended was close by, too, as were shops and a movie theatre. It was a great location, convenient to all public transportation. We lived there for five years until my parents were able to purchase their first and only home, a bungalow on the southwest side of Chicago.

Although we did not have much, we made the best of what we had. We often received hand-me-downs from relatives in Michigan. I remember looking forward to receiving their packages, filled with used clothing and other items. Another older cousin would provide us with outgrown toys and games. One year she gave us her old bicycle. What a nice treat that was!

At Christmas, Mother always managed to be able to have gifts for us. She would shop early and put clothes and toys on layaway plans. Most of the toys would have all our names on them so we could all receive a lot of gifts. Dad always managed to get a real tree. Sometimes it would be just a day or two before Christmas when prices would drop. But we did not mind. My sisters and I enjoyed getting out the decorations and trimming the tree. We would make a mess; getting tinsel all over the carpet and sweeping it up was always a chore. My sister Sharon would read The Night Before Christmas and lead us into Christmas carols. Miracle on 34th Street and White Christmas were our favorite Christmas movies. We always made Christmas Cards for our parents using glitter and other decorative items.

Holiday dinners were festive occasions for us. Grandpa and Grandma would spend all day and night. The kitchen was always busy with cooking food, and other family members would join us later for dinner. At Christmas time we celebrated the Feast of the Seven Fishes on the eve of Christmas. We had buckets of fresh clams and muscle. The cod fish we used was imported from the Mediterranean Sea, packed in salt to preserve it. We had to soak it for days to get the salt out. The table was always full of Italian pastries, nuts, fresh fruit, and wine. Mother would let us open one Christmas gift each from one of our relatives. It was usually pajamas, socks, or slippers. We were happy to receive them, although a toy or game would have excited us more.

I am the third daughter born to my parents. My sister Sharon was the firstborn. Two years later, Janice arrived. Dad wanted a son so much that they did not wait too long before I was born fourteen months later. Mother now had three young daughters to take care of, and we were a handful. They decided to wait before trying again for a son. Four years later my brother Ed was born, and then my brother John three years after that.

As a toddler, I was happy and gregarious, always wanting to be playful. My sister Janice was more reserved and did not like my aggressiveness. She was always biting me to keep me away. But that's not unusual behavior, I understand, from a toddler who now had to share attention.

Mother started introducing domestic chores to us at the age of five. That is the age a child begins attending kindergarten. I was jealous that my two older sisters got to help with the laundry and ironing, dusting and sweeping, and helping with meals. To me it was like playing house, and I wanted to play, too. Mother was tired of hearing me complain, so she would allow me to participate in some of the easier chores. It was fun pretending that I was grown up. But, eventually, the newness of being grown up wore off. Mother told me that my enthusiasm in doing things was why Grandma wanted me to stay with her during Grandpa's procedure.

I was a happy child. Life seemed so simple then. We had our chores to do when not in school, but we also had time to play with our neighborhood friends and each other. We spent most of our time playing outdoors. It got us out of Mother's way so she could attend to the cooking and cleaning. We were glad to get out and play the usual childhood games of hide and seek, hopscotch, jump rope, and even marbles with our friends. My sisters and I had dolls, of course, and played house. But we also had to watch our younger brothers, so we played cowboys and Indians, a lot with Ed, and wheeled John in the stroller. On rainy days we would play on the back porch. It had a big bench swing where we would snuggle with a blanket and tell spooky stories. In the summer the fire department would open the hydrants for a little while and let us play in the water. Sometimes they would place a board across the opening to create a waterfall. One of the neighborhood boys made a skateboard and attached a wooden crate to it. I remember sitting inside the crate when he would run it through the waterfall. That was always a lot of fun. In the winter months, we played cards and board games or worked on puzzles after our chores. Mother believed in getting us all into bed early, before 7:00 p.m. I never went to bed without my friend Jesus. He was always tucked in the mirror above the dresser, watching over me.

CHAPTER 3

Jesus became my secret friend. I took Him with me everywhere I went. I did not share the relationship I had with Him. He was my friend. I talked to Him daily and consulted with Him when I faced fears or challenges. A child's mind is simple. I would bring my problem-solving to Jesus with the promise of doing something for Him. I was confident that He could solve any problem I had. After all, He took away my fear at Grandma's. So, I became a negotiator. If I wanted a special favor or something from my sisters or brothers, I would promise to take on one of their chores or commit to playing a game with them. And so, this is how I was with Jesus. When I needed His help, I would promise to kiss His picture a hundred times and obey my mother or do something I really did not want to do but knew that it would please Him.

I cannot explain the special bond I had with my new secret friend. When I wanted to talk to Him or negotiate something I needed, I would take His picture to the bathroom, and behind a closed door, I would whisper my want or need. I would then kiss His picture as many times as I felt my request warranted…anywhere from one hundred to five hundred times. Then, I would return the picture to the mirror. He became a trusted friend. Someone I could count on.

My relationship with Jesus did not mean I was not a normal child, misbehaving like most children my age, but I always knew He was watching my behavior and disapproving of my sinful ways when I would tell those little "white" lies. Fearful that He would leave me for my actions, I would confess my sorrows of letting Him down, promising to be better, and would always end with kissing His picture hundreds of times. I am sure you are thinking…how silly!

While my grandmother brought Jesus into my life as a friend, He was not a stranger to me before that. We attended church as children and looked forward to our Bible study classes and church friends. We learned all about Jesus through the stories in the Bible. We were taught the Lord's prayer and others. Up until this point, to me, He was a character in a book. But that night at Grandma's, Jesus came to life.

◊

Eventually, I outgrew the silliness of kissing His picture. My relationship with Him matured as

I did. Unfortunately, with my maturity, I developed independence. I still had Jesus in my life, but my communication with Him was not throughout the day, every day, as it used to be. Some days, it would only be at night when I would say my bedtime prayers and share my day.

One day, while I was in high school, Jesus called me back. I was fifteen years old, and I was on locker guard duty. One of the girls, who was changing into her gym suit and getting ready for gym, said something to another girl that was so kind and sincere. I was impressed by her actions and thought, I want to be like that, genuinely kind and giving. My thoughts soon became verbal, and I began speaking to Jesus, asking Him for that kind of heart. I wanted to be like that girl. Suddenly I felt a sensation take over my body. It was the warmth of an embrace. I did not realize it at the time, but what I was asking is that I wanted Jesus to come into my heart. I wanted a loving heart like Jesus. I became a different person. I yearned to be with Him again. I started looking for ways to spend private time with Him.

I started attending church again. A school friend invited me to join her at her church, which was just a block from our home. I was glad to be back at church. When we moved from the two-flat to my parent's new home, it was difficult for us to continue going to the church that I had attended since childhood. Public transportation was not that convenient. There were no direct routes.

Returning to church gave me time to spend with Jesus. Private time with Jesus was not easy when you were living in a small bungalow house with two younger brothers and two older sisters. Sneaking private time meant going to the bathroom. It was the only room in the house where you could be totally alone behind a closed door. And, even then, someone would be knocking on it, wondering when you would be coming out. I remember my family kidding me about the time I spent in there.

One night I went to bed after my sister Janice. We shared the same bedroom. My older sister Sharon was now living on her own in her own apartment. Janice was already asleep when I got into bed. The room was dark, with a small stream of light coming from the bedroom door, which was ajar. I closed my eyes to say my prayers. When I opened them again, the room was dimly lit by the light coming from the window. The neighbor next door was in their bathroom that faced my bedroom. It was giving off some light that made it easy to see the contents of the room. Small bungalow houses built in the city were on small lots with eight to ten feet between them. So, the light was bright, almost like a lit lamp. The curtains on the window kept the brightness out, giving off a dim light.

I lay awake a long time, examining the room, thinking how their bathroom light lit up the bedroom and how much brighter it would be without the curtains. Finally, after thirty to forty minutes, the light went out, and the room was dark again. As the evenings passed, I noticed the light would come on about the same time every night, 11:00 p.m.

One night, I could not sleep. I said my prayers, rambling on with a lot of detail to make the time pass, when I decided to get up and check out the light at the window. I was right. The brightness was greater when the curtains were opened.

I took one of the religious books we had and brought it to the window. The light was bright enough to see the words clearly. I started flipping through the pages when something caught my eye. The book was a Catholic schoolbook. I'm not sure how we got the book. We did not attend a Catholic school. It had a lot of prayers in it. One was a bedtime prayer: "Mathew, Mark, Luke and John, bless this bed that I lay on. Before I lay me down to sleep, I give my soul to Christ to keep, etc." I read it over and over. I felt like I drifted off into another world of peace and joy. The sort of feeling one gets when they are in church worshipping. Every night after that, I would go to bed at the same time and wait for the neighbor's bathroom light to go on so I could read that book and memorize the prayers. This became my quiet time with Jesus. I did this for many months. Sneaking around to spend time with my secret friend. I never shared my renewed relationship with Jesus with anyone, although it was becoming obvious to a few that I was changing. My father was the first to notice it.

CHAPTER 4

D ad was a machinist working for Western Electric. He had many opportunities to move up in the company but never wanted the responsibilities tied to the job. He was a perfectionist, and his rewards were in the finished product of what he made. He was a company man who never took a day off and would work many overtime hours on a Saturday to accommodate and please the boss. He would much prefer to go fishing on Saturday with his brother and sons, but if the boss wanted him to work, he would. Dad was a simple man. His idea of living was to get married, raise a family, and live comfortably. Yet, he was also very knowledgeable on many subjects. He read the newspaper almost daily for current events, and he loved to read the encyclopedia.

Many nights, Dad would come home from work at 1:00–2:00 a.m. He worked the 3:00–11:00 p.m. shift. Not driving, he would have to rely on the bus schedules, and at that hour, they would only run every half hour or hour. He would also stop at a local tavern to have a beer or two with some of the guys. Many nights he would come home inebriated, and he would be loud and amorous, wanting attention. Everyone in the house would be sleeping at that hour. Mother was now working late hours herself. She would come home, have a bite to eat, attend to a few chores, and retire for the night. I was usually up. I am now a senior in high school, focusing on art as a college major. My art projects would keep me working late hours. I was also working for a large retail chain after school, putting in, on average, thirty hours per week, when working Saturdays. It was not unusual for me to start my school homework at 11:00 p.m.

I spent a lot of time with Dad during these late hours. I would cook his dinner, and we would talk about all kinds of things, but mostly about life. I would tell him we wished he were around more. That we loved and missed him. He would critique my art assignments and give me pointers. For the next year and a half, Dad and I became late-night companions. I know my kindness and the attention I gave to him made a difference. One night, my mother was still up when Dad came home. I was just finishing up an assignment and decided to go to bed so they could be alone. I said my good nights and went to bed. With the bedroom door ajar, I heard Dad say to Mother, "You know, Babe, there's something different about her. I can't put my finger on it."

Unfortunately, the change in me came with a price. It ruined my relationship with my sister, Janice. Our teenage years were not as close as they could have been. I was becoming closer to Jesus, focusing on Him. My siblings saw my actions as buttering up to my parents, but I was just being what Jesus wanted me to be. Kind, loving, and obedient. My actions were effortless. They just came naturally because I had Jesus in my heart. Dad was not the only one who could see what was happening. Other people were noticing it as well.

One day, my great Aunt Carmella came to visit my mother. I happened to be home with Mother that day. It was just the three of us. We were sitting around the dinette table having coffee and a Danish when Aunt Carmella started talking Italian to my mother. I knew this must be something she did not want me to hear; otherwise, she would have spoken in English. While she was talking to my mother, she kept looking at me and smiling. I finally said, "Okay what are you two talking about?" Mother replied, "Your aunt says you are always happy. That there is a spirit about you."

"That's Jesus," I said.

Mother said, "She knows." My mother told me later that my Aunt Carmella had her own personal relationship with Jesus.

Another time, at work, a man referred to me as a Christian to another lady. I never wore a cross or even mentioned God, Christ, Jesus, or religion in the workplace. He came to that conclusion on his own by my actions. Jesus gave me that kind, loving spirit I had asked for back in the locker room when I was fifteen. In fact, my high school yearbook has many written notations from classmates and teachers saying, "Stay as nice and sweet as you are."

I am not perfect. I have made bad choices. But Jesus always forgave me and never left me. He is the most loyal, dependable friend anyone can ask for. And, like any other friend who truly cares about you, He lets you know when you are making bad decisions. Unfortunately, we do not always listen.

&

I got married at the age of nineteen. I met my first husband in college. We both attended an evening class, Science of Art. It was a fill-in course for him. I was majoring in Art with a minor in Business. On our first date, he asked me to marry him. We were immediately attracted to one another. Our family backgrounds were similar. He was raised in an Italian home like I was. We shared the same traditions and loved the same kinds of foods. We were deeply in love and perfect for one another. My parents were in shock when I told them we wanted to get married within the next three months, before the end of the year. My husband-to-be wanted the tax deduction. They were concerned I would drop out of school, become pregnant, and ruin all my chances of having a career. While in college, I was modeling for a large retail store and in a training program for management. I had hopes of becoming part of their advertising team or as a buyer in their purchasing department. So, I could understand their concerns.

I loved my parents, and I did not want to do anything that would make them unhappy or ruin my relationship with them. I brought my concerns to Jesus. What was I to do? I was in love, and I felt in my heart that this was the right man for me. He was four years older than I was and mature, with a promising career. He was in the Air Force Reserve and working for a nationally known company in their distribution warehouse as the accountant while attending evening college courses to obtain his CPA. Having met his parents and sister, I felt it was a perfect match. We both wanted to be together. We were ready for marriage. I was always obedient to my parents, but delaying my marriage was taking a risk that I did not want to take. So, I listened to my heart and Jesus, praying that I was making the right decision, and went against my parents' wishes and got married.

We were married twenty-three years, and in those years, my parents and family grew to accept our marriage, recognizing that I had made the right decision. During those years I never shared with my husband the relationship I had with my secret friend. We were not a regular church-going couple, and I was embarrassed at my age to have him find out that I communicated with an invisible being. So, Jesus stayed a secret friend, and my time with Him remained private, bedtime prayers and conversations when I was alone.

Was I really embarrassed about my relationship with Jesus, or was I still being selfish to want to keep Jesus all to myself? God had a plan to change all that.

CHAPTER 5

My first marriage ended in divorce. It was a turning point in my life. But, because of it, God enabled me to come out of the "closet" and share the close, long-standing relationship that I had with Jesus all these years with my family and friends for the first time. I began attending church each Sunday again, which allowed me to talk openly about my relationship with Jesus and to express my love for Him. I rededicated my life and was baptized.

The woman helping me disrobe and prepare for the baptism encouraged me to embrace my new life and allow God to lead me to do His work. I listened to her words of wisdom, and, like a good student, I put them into action.

The first step I took was to learn to tithe. I had heard about tithing but never really understood its meaning, purpose, or value. So, this was a difficult lesson for me. My parents taught me to be a saver. Spending money on something not tangible or beneficial with some type of monetary reward went against my upbringing. Tithing, to me, was not a necessary expense. It was a type of gift. With that thought in mind, I was prepared to give to the church an amount of money I was willing to part with that would not affect my budget. Then I learned that God wanted 10 percent of my earnings. This really took creativity as I had a set budget already in place, but I began giving 10 percent of my net earnings. Finally, I surrendered and gave 10 percent of my gross income, and the blessings were endless. God wanted me to be obedient to His word. And when I was, He blessed me. Over time, I came to really understand tithing, which provides the funds needed to support your church. It was a way of giving back to God.

Getting involved in an outreach program was my next step. My church participated in Evangelism Explosion, which is a training for outreach evangelizing. I studied that for months and became qualified to evangelize each week with a small group of others who studied and graduated from the course. Sharing salvation with others became easy for me, and I used the skills we were equipped with to evangelize whenever I felt God was telling me to.

Most everyone believes in a God, but not everyone knows about salvation and that it is a Free gift for everyone to receive who accepts Jesus as their Lord and Savior. I wanted everyone to know about this Free gift and about Eternal Life, so I began sharing my good news with everyone who would listen.

But words are not always the best way to communicate God's love. The phrase "actions speak louder than words" is so true. My actions as a young girl revealed my relationship with Jesus, not my words. If you are looking for ways to share God's love, I can tell you from my experience that God will provide opportunities for you, especially when you pray the Jabez Prayer, asking God to enlarge your territory.

1 Chronicles 4:10

I remember the first time I prayed the Jabez prayer. Everyone in the Home Bible Study group warned me to be prepared. "God will start using you in a mighty way," they said. They were right. I call my first experience a test of faith and obedience.

ಂ

I was at the grocery store. It was mid-afternoon during a weekday, and the store and parking lot were not that busy. I was there to buy a few items. This was not my regular shopping day. As I was leaving the store and entering the parking lot, a man approached me. He was a young man with a slender build, dark hair that needed cutting, and a short beard from not shaving. He asked if I could give him some money for food. I was not in the habit of giving people money.

Occasionally, I would give a few dollars to a beggar at a stop light. I never wanted to encourage someone to use the money for a sinful act. This young man was different from others who I had been approached by. I told him I was happy to buy him some food and asked if he would come with me back to the grocery store.

As we went down the aisles, he stopped at the soup section to buy instant soup packages. He picked up the smaller package, put it down, and then picked up the larger package. He looked at it and began to put it back on the shelf, reaching for the smaller package again. I said, "Take the larger package. It will give you more meals." He looked at me and shook his head and took the larger package. He then went to the tea section to buy some tea bags. Again, I encouraged him to take the larger package. I thought to myself, these are not the usual purchases a person would buy. They are compact and only need hot water that can easily be gotten at any gas station or convenience store. This must be a homeless man.

As we started walking toward the check-out counter, I asked him if he wanted some sandwiches or fruit or anything else. He said, "No." that was all he wanted. I paid for his purchase, and we headed toward the door. He thanked me and turned to walk in the opposite direction of where I was headed to get to my car. I took a few steps and turned to watch where he would go. He was nowhere in sight. He disappeared!

Walking back to my car, I started talking to Jesus. Was this a test of obedience? Was God testing me to see if I would listen to Him when He needed me to be there for Him? My mind started thinking. When we pray to God for help, He does not come down from the sky to help us. He sends his Angels or someone to help. Was I to be someone God could rely on to help others when needed? What a blessing and honor that would be.

It felt good to help that man. For whatever reason he needed my help, and I was glad to be there for him. I thanked God for that opportunity and continued to pray the Jabez prayer, asking God to enlarge my territory. This meant keeping a keen ear to hear God when he needed me again. It was not long after that experience that God chose me for another chance to help someone in need.

I started to leave the new house that I was having built when I noticed a Fed-X package leaning against the front door. I put it in the car and started driving home. At the first red light, I reached for the package and opened it. There was a $1,400 check inside with a letter from the insurance company, stating it was a refund of overpayment. That an adjustment to the premium was made. I thought, Oh great, I can use this for purchasing something for the house. My mind began to think of all the different things I could buy. Suddenly, there was a thump in my heart. I gasped and said, "Oh no, this check is not meant for me, is it? I kept driving and talking out loud to Jesus, looking for answers. I finally reached home, pulled into the garage, and entered the kitchen. My mother was staying with me at this time, and she greeted me. She began whispering that someone was here to see me. She asked if I was expecting this person. I said, "No. I have no appointments." I put my purse and Fed-X envelope down and walked into the living room.

Sitting on the sofa was a lady I had met in one of my network groups. She and her husband owned a small cleaning company. Her husband was not a very responsible person. She shared with me that he had failed to pay the rent for the last two months and that the landlord was about to evict them. She was able to come up with most of the money but was seven hundred dollars short. She prayed to God for help, and He put my name in her head. She knew where I lived because they did some cleaning for me the previous year. She said she kept talking to God to be sure He wanted her to come to see me. God convinced her to do it, so she did. She was very apologetic and asked if I could help her. I shared my Fed-X story with her, and we looked at each other wide-eyed. I wrote her a check for seven hundred dollars. Then I laughed when I realized that God had split the check amount in two. Seven hundred dollars for her and seven hundred for me!

After she left, I thanked God for the opportunity to help her and shared the story with my mother. Mother was concerned that I would never get the money back. I told her it was never meant to be my money. God had blessed me with seven hundred dollars. She said, "Peggy, you're something else!" When you are communicating with God daily, there is no fear to following Jesus. For me, it was easy to part with the seven hundred dollars because I already had a giving heart like Jesus. The next assignment God gave me was not so easy.

&

I am a mortgage broker. Today they call us loan originators. I am self-employed and working from my home, helping people with home mortgages. Most of my clients are referred to me by other satisfied customers or business owners with whom I network. I received a call from an investor who owned ten investment properties that he rented out. It was right at the time of the real estate crash.

The year is 2008.

This investor needs cash to pay the property taxes on all ten of the properties. He has equity in one of the properties that could be refinanced; however, with the impending real estate crash, loan programs that were once available to investors are now gone. My lenders have all turned him down. He does manage to find someone who will refinance the one property with equity, but the funds will not be available until a week after the property taxes are due. His call to me is at 10:00 a.m., the day the taxes had to be paid. He wants me to personally lend him $40,000. He needs to have the money by 2:00 p.m.

There is this thump in my heart again. The same kind of thump I felt when God told me the $1,400 check was not mine to keep. I told the investor that I would have to call him back in an hour. I hung up the phone, put my head in my hands, and started talking to God. "$40,000 is a lot of money," I said. "I know he only wants it for a week. He will pay it back when his loan closes and funds, but it is a lot of money to lose if something happens. I can have him sign a promissory note, tie the debt to one of his properties, and record it." On and on I go, talking to God. Finally, I said, "Jesus, you need to give me a clear sign that this is what you want me to do."

A half-hour later, the doorbell rang. It is a courier service delivering a package of mortgage documents to me. I signed for the package and started to close the door. The man delivering the package takes a few steps and turns around and says, "I don't know what this means, lady, but God just told me to tell you it's going to be alright." I said, "What?" He said, "God just told me to tell you it is going to be alright." We looked at each other. He looked puzzled, and I was temporarily paralyzed. We said our goodbyes again, and I went to the phone to call the investor. "Meet me at my bank in one hour," I said. God sent me his answer.

At the bank, the banker thought I was crazy, lending this man money using one of his properties as collateral during those turbulent times in real estate. I had no fear. I knew Jesus was protecting me. One week later, the investor sent me a check for $40,000. I never charged him a fee for my services or interest for the borrowed money.

I stopped praying the Jabez prayer for a long time after that, but God was not going to let me off that easily. He still thumps at my heart, and I still respond. There are a lot of stories to share. I call them God stories.

Listening to God and helping others is only part of the relationship I have with Jesus. Talking and praying to Him is the best part–fellowship.

CHAPTER 6

Best friends are hard to find. It takes work to develop good, solid relationships. But, when you find a good friend, they are like gold. You love everything about them. You want to have them around all the time to talk and laugh with. Sharing every minute of your day with them fills your heart. Jesus is that kind of friend to me.

I am not a little girl anymore, running to Jesus because I am afraid of the dark or because I am afraid to face a difficult decision. There is no need for me to do that because He is with me everywhere I go. He is with me when I am driving in my car, keeping me safe, and He is with me when I am working and need to make those important decisions. And He is even with me when I am just doing house chores and cooking. And as with most friends, my relationship with Jesus is not one-sided. When I talk to Him in prayer, He responds.

My first real test of faith through prayer came when I was asked to give an investor $40,000 to pay his property taxes. I have prayed a lot over the years, waiting for immediate responses like the kind I received the day I prayed for an answer to help the investor. In my heart I wanted to help the man, but I also wanted to be sure it was the wise thing to do. So, I went to Jesus for an answer and confirmation.

My second test of real faith came weeks later when my cat became ill, and I was waiting for the veterinarian to give me the prognosis.

I am a cat lover and not very fond of dogs, probably because when I was growing up, we had a French poodle who was very temperamental and bit everyone in our household. He was given to us by a family member. I believe the dog had a difficult time adjusting to a family of five children when coming from a family of one child and a more peaceful environment. We were all happy when my mother found a more suitable home for the dog.

They say that cats are independent creatures, although I have not found that to be true with any of my cats over the years. Cats and dogs can become a product of their environment, just like humans. My cat, Nefertiti, was unique. I saved her from an animal shelter along with another cat, Cleopatra. Cleopatra was six months old and already named. Nefertiti was eight weeks old and needed a name as royal as Cleopatra. She had a pure white belly with dark black and silver stripes on her back. She could sit on her hind legs like a dog and beg. I called her my praying cat because she would put her front paws together when begging as if to be praying. She was smart and loving. Very much a lap cat. We were very close. I am sure every cat owner could brag about their cat as well.

One day Nefertiti became ill. She was only five years old. She would not eat or drink. I became worried and took her to the veterinarian. He was fearful she might have a tumor. I asked that if it was a tumor, could it be removed with surgery, and would she survive? He said, "I will not know that until I open her up to see what we are working with. I will call you with my findings."

I drove home thinking how I would miss having Nefertiti around. I loved her so. She was young. I was not emotionally prepared to lose her. I pleaded with God not to take her from me. I was not ready to accept losing her. When I got home, I could not work. I paced the floor, praying for hours, finding myself negotiating with God as I had when I was a child. I need more time with her so that I can accept and adjust to her loss. Please God, I begged, give me six more months.

Two or more hours passed, and no word from the doctor. "This cannot be good news," I said to myself. "I must call and find out what is happening." The doctor told me he had been trying to reach me for over an hour. It was a tumor, and he needed to know if I wanted it removed. It would not save her life, but it would give her another six months or longer. And he was not sure if the surgery would be successful since he had had her open for over an hour, trying to reach me. It would be a miracle. Nefertiti survived the surgery and lived for six months. Exactly six months! God answered my prayer.

Communicating with God through prayer is believing that He is there with you listening. If you are praying with the mindset that your prayer will not get answered, then it probably will not. My faith and belief that God would respond in His way and His time always got me through those times I needed help. And, sometimes, we never recognize that our prayers are being answered because we are hoping for different results.

But when you are communicating with God daily you become aware of His presence. You can see His hand in everything you say and do. You recognize that the events in your life are not by accident. Sometimes the roads we travel are smooth and joyful, and sometimes, the roads are bumpy and difficult to navigate. If that is an example of your life, do not be fooled…each step you take is carefully planned for you. The bumpy roads are there to make you stronger and to rely on Him more. The smooth roads are blessings for obedience.

In the Garden of Eden, God loved being with Adam and Eve. He enjoyed their companionship and the time they spent together. God yearns for our love and companionship. He is our heavenly father who wants to help us navigate our life on earth just as our birth father. Would you go days, weeks, or months without talking to your earthly father? What kind of a relationship would you have? When I make God part of my daily life, I can hear His laughter as I go about my day, and I can feel His warm embrace when I need a reassuring hug or comfort. He will never leave you. It is you who will drift away from Him.

CHAPTER 7

My mother came to live with me when she was diagnosed with lung cancer. Part of her lung was removed by surgery, and she required daily radiation treatments. It was a blessing to have her live with me. I was able to spend every day with her, something I was not able to do for twenty years since I had moved away from Chicago.

My father passed away a few years prior to her living with me. His death was a great personal loss to her. I can only imagine the heartbreak she went through. They were married for over fifty years, with all the ups and downs most long-term marriages go through. Their retirement years brought them the most joy. They got to travel, visiting family and friends. And while finances were always a challenge raising their family, that was not the case during their golden years.

I was happy and proud to introduce Mother to all my friends, church family, and Bible study group. They all had local families that I got to know and love. So, when Mother moved in with me, I wanted everyone to love Mother as I did. She was kind-hearted, with a gentle nature. Occasionally, she would show her Italian spitfire, but that was rare.

We took family trips together where she was able to experience her first trip on a cruise. But the highlight of her travel was including her children on a trip to Italy, where she could see where her parents lived, which fulfilled her life's dream.

Mother had a zest for life. She loved her family. She was strong in her family traditions. When diagnosed with lung cancer, she had a positive attitude that it would be removed and that she would live a long life to enjoy with her family. Her positive outlook was encouraging to me. I began to believe that she would beat it. That God would give her what she wanted, a long life. She was in excellent health outside of the cancer. She would walk miles a day or an hour on the treadmill. She ate healthy foods all her life before it became popular to eat healthy. She was a great inspiration.

The cancer was in remission for two years. When it came back, I could see her optimism fade. I could also see that God would be taking her from me. My heart was breaking, but I knew all my prayers could not change what God had already planned for her life. He was calling her home to be with Him. He gave her to me for three years, which is the time she lived after her diagnosis. One day, she shared with me her thoughts. "I'm at the end of my road," she said, looking sad with a far-off gaze. I said, "No, Mother. You're at a fork in the road, and it is time for you to take another road. That road is going to lead you to eternal life. No more sadness or pain. It will be a uniting of family and friends that you have not seen for a long time. Dad will be waiting for you. It will be an awesome journey. One that I would take with you hand in hand if God were to bless us with that." She looked at me and smiled.

During those last few months, we spent hours talking about family and her life. It was at this time that she shared a story with me that I had never heard before.

ೋ

When I was an infant and my parents were living in the apartment above the store, my mother decided to go to the movies to take a break from her routine of house chores. She took my two older sisters to the movies with her. Before she left the apartment, she told my father that I was running a low fever and that he should look after me; I was sleeping in the crib.

When she returned from the movies several hours later, she went to see how I was doing. I was purple and blue, fighting to breathe. She shouted for my father to call for help, and a few minutes later, the fire department arrived. They tried to clear my lungs, but it was too late. They said they could not save me. My father grabbed me and started to breathe life back in me. Minutes later, I came back to life. She told me how bad my father felt that he did not watch over me more carefully; and, that after that day, I became attached to

Dad as if to show my gratefulness for giving me back my life. She said as an infant, I would not fall asleep until he came home from work in the early morning hours. I had to hear his voice before I would fall asleep.

I asked her why she never told me this story before. She said she did not see any reason to mention it. "We didn't lose you and that's what is important."

℘

Is it unusual for a young child to be so attached to a portrait of a man who she came to believe in and trust as a friend? Is it possible that the face she saw on the 8" x 10" embossed glossy picture was one she had seen before? That it was a familiar face. A face attached to a person who, for one brief moment while she was fighting to breathe as an infant, showed her His love and kindness.

One day, she will know for sure.

LIFE'S JOURNEY

Life is a journey
You cannot predict your fate.
It begins with God's creation,
A day to celebrate.

He loves you from that moment,
And yearns to be your friend.
He smiles down upon you,
And whispers follow me to the end.

He will bring you joy and laughter,
When you travel along together.
You need not ever be afraid,
For He will guide and protect you forever.

The roads may be bumpy
As you march in time,
But the journey will be worth it.
You are the flower on a vine.

Then you will soar high into the clouds
Like a bird with wings,
To a faraway place
Where all the angels sing.

Peggy Watrous Walters

www.ingramcontent.com/pod-product-compliance
Lightning Source LLC
Chambersburg PA
CBHW040157160726
48006CB00014B/1794